MW01114006

FACTORS

of Transformation

FACTORS

of Transformation
BE THE CHANGE YOU WANT

Dr. Keith L. Marshall, Psy.D

Noahs Ark Publishing
Beverly Hills, California

Factors of Transformation: Be the Change You Want

ISBN 978-0-578-78645-2

Copyright (c) 2020 by Keith Lamont Marshall

Published by:

Noahs Ark Publishing Service

www.noahsarkpublishing.com

Editor: Elyse Wietstock

Graphic Design: Christopher C. White

Interior Design: James Sparkman

To my wife Lilly, who gracefully and tirelessly worked to help me improve my life, and who prayed for me in my weakest and darkest moments.

To my Father in Heaven, for His Grace and Mercy. And to my family for their love and support, especially my mother, my wife, my brothers Kenny and Kevin, and my sister-in-law Aisha.

CONTENTS

INTRODUCTION

Factors of Transformation: Be the Change You Want is a collection of ten key factors I developed to help you maintain a sense of balance and synchronicity in your life. I want you to understand the power of your conscious and unconscious thoughts in every dimension of your life, whether that is spiritual, mental, emotional, physical, or social. The idea is to help you achieve liberation from negative thinking patterns that yield poor behaviors, and to become sensitive to the power of your thoughts so that you can become more productive. Young or old, the goal is the same; be the change you want to see in the world. Understand that every dimension of your existence must be intentional if your unique potential as a person is going to be realized and sustained in a healthy manner.

In my book *Faith To Freedom: From Dumpster to Doctor*, I shared how I overcame childhood sexual and physical abuse. Over twenty-three years of chronic crack cocaine addiction, I was homeless, lived behind dumpsters and abandoned buildings, and went in and out of jails and institutions. I was shot in the head, stabbed multiple times, and left to die! Through these hardships I became spiritually aware and conscious. I learned I had to practice principles in all my affairs; I considered every dimension of my life and changed the self-destructive thinking and behaviors that hurt me and others around me. I was able to tap into my potential and the gifts that I often unconsciously underestimated in my past. Today I am a Doctor of Psychology, Author, Owner and CEO of my own company, and living a more enduring, useful, and productive life.

Life is short, one thing that ties us together is the reality that we must accept life as it unfolds no matter how it unfolds. There is no time to waste because you are not guaranteed tomorrow. *Factors of Transformation: Be the Change You Want* details how faulty and unconscious beliefs affect your mind, body, and spirit. This short and simple read will encourage your potential and help you to experience the great and unique gifts inside of you. Your self-talk and perceptions should be in line with your "truth" when you are seeking to live out your purpose. When you underestimate your potential, often it is some form of "stinking thinking" driving your feelings and behavior. Instead of simply *reacting* to life, this book will give you the insight to help you *respond* to life with purpose.

Why wait to make changes in your life when you are not guaranteed to live another day? Why not be in touch with your mind, body, spirit, and relationships *today?* At the very least, be the best "you" today. It is easy for your thoughts, especially unconscious thoughts, to either promote or destroy growth in your life. You can look at your life today and examine your emotional, physical, and spiritual state, as well as your relationships with others. Ask yourself, "Are all the areas of my life healthy, or am I trying to achieve a healthier life in my mind, body, and spirit?" Do you need any improvement? Does your thinking support your well-being in all areas of your life? *Factors of Transformation* will give you some insight about each dimension and help you determine where you may need to improve.

In most cases, we are our own worst enemy. We are driven by our feelings and not by healthy transformational thinking. I may not have all the answers, but no one can dispute the importance of applying consistent principles when you want to transform your life.

Chapter One
"YOU ARE MORE THAN YOUR BODY"

If you do not believe in God, a Higher Power, or you are an Atheist or Agnostic, trust me you are not alone. For many years, I was turned off by church. I saw greedy and selfish pastors, and self-righteous people who preached about "Jesus" or "Allah", yet continued to see the speck in everyone else's eye and not the wickedness in their own hearts. It is not my job to convince you who or what God is, or what God means to you. I am not going to apologize for my belief in God.

God does not need my help to convince you or draw you to Him. He is big and mighty enough to do that Himself. However, if you read my book *Faith to Freedom: From Dumpster to Doctor*, you will surely see how I got out of debating society about my belief in God and having problems with God. It never dawned on me why I was questioning, cynical, and non-believing in God. If I am keeping it real, I didn't think about it because He was not doing what I wanted Him to do for me. I never once asked myself, *"I wonder if God was having problems with me."* We can truly be ugly and selfish as people, and want to blame the Creator for all the problems of this world when in fact we messed up the gift of free will. The pride and arrogance (stinking thinking) to not even consider that we were created to love and respect each other is the sickness of the human condition. Our dilemma has nothing to do with who we are on the outside, though our behaviors are what we see; it has everything to do with who we are on the inside, these fragile vessels we call "bodies."

If you have not realized my meaning with this first factor—and I am not trying to be sarcastic— you probably know that you are surely not the "Creator", and I guarantee at some point in your life, as with every other human being walking the face of this earth, you have asked questions like "Where am I going when I die?", "Is there an afterlife?", "Is there life after death?", "Who is God?", "Is there even such a thing as God, or some Higher Power?", "Do I just vanish and that's it?" Have you asked yourself these or similar questions? I can assure you that after you read the next nine key factors you will agree they all are connected, and if you are honest you will know that "you are not just your body."

Each morning before you do anything, connect with the Creator first. In prayer and meditation thank Him for another day. Ask for help with your thoughts, your words, and your actions throughout the day ahead. Pray for protection over those you love, and ask for mercy for people less fortunate than you are. Pray even when you do not feel like it. Remember that your feelings are byproducts of your thinking, which may or may not be correct. For example, if you believe you are not worthy of the Creator's forgiveness, and simply won't pray or acknowledge Him, you're stuck in stinking thinking and cannot develop spiritually or grow. If you avoid spiritual development, beat yourself up, and internalize shame and guilt, those feelings will invariably manifest in your behaviors at some point.

Let your first contact with the Creator be a practice you do no matter what you are thinking, feeling, or doing. He made you, so pray without ceasing; be grateful even when times are tough or you feel bad or guilty. The idea here is to first acknowledge your need for God to help you fix your inner self, and be right within before any positive changes can be made in your life.

Seek His purpose by reading the bible, meditation books, fellowship with others who are principle driven, and be open to correction and taking direction. Change will require you to take action no matter how you feel. You must have the same consistency of action and purpose that you had when practicing old behaviors that keep you restless, irritable, and discontented (RID). You must reconcile the reality that you are not your body, but a spirit within your body.

Be sure to seek the counsel and help of others and be open to new ideas. After all, the Creator uses people and situations to help us. If we can be humble enough to smash our egos, admit that we do not know it all, and be willing to take direction from principle-driven people such as pastors, counselors, therapists, friends, and advisors who show love and respect for themselves and others in their actions, there is no doubt that positive and enduring changes can be made in our lives. I will not apologize for my belief in God and our Savior Jesus Christ, but this book is not trying to convince you to follow that same belief. My purpose is to get you to ponder your thoughts and feelings on the most important dimension (your spirit) and at the very least think about your belief in a Higher Power. To become spiritually aware, you must be open-minded to this reality. Human pride and self-will live on the same "stinking thinking" road. A road to disaster and definite failure.

Become willing to trust at least one person and share your

real experiences so you can develop the ability to test and walk in the truth of any event that causes you to be restless, irritable, and discontented, so you can better respond and not simply react. Coping with life can be extremely hard sometimes, however it is no excuse to self-destruct or hurt others. If you are spiritually fit and feel secure in your place in the universe, you will be more aware of your feelings and how they relate to your actions, and can better avoid hurting yourself or others.

Genesis 1:27–So God created man in his own image, in the image of God he created him; male and female he created them. Since Our Heavenly Father made us, He knows what is best for us and the purpose for which He made us. It would be wise to go to the source from which I came to get direction about what my human purpose is. Our dilemma is that we have self will and the freedom to choose. Unfortunately our flesh is weak and has an insatiable appetite for serving itself. That is why practicing principles is most difficult and seeking power greater than you through prayer is necessary. Practicing principles will be extremely uncomfortable in the beginning, especially emotionally.

Philippians 4:13–I can do all things through him who strengthens me. When I look back on my life, I find that my fears of both the unknown inner world (i.e., the subconscious) and the external world around me controlled my actions. In my book *Faith To Freedom* I talked about how I manipulated to get my way, most often with women. What I discovered was these actions were the result of my faulty beliefs that I was not "good enough." The ways I tried to compensate for being uncomfortable with myself or to avoid feeling that discomfort, such as drugs, sex, lying, and manipulating, seemed at the time to have more power than surrendering to the real power, which is from my Creator.

It never dawned on me to seek God's will and rely on His strength while I pressed on to discover myself and the purpose that was laid out for me. I now recognize that my human suffering was allowed to happen as an act of love from the Creator, to force me into a level of humility so I could receive His strength to overcome my obstacles. My obstacles were undoubtedly driven from within (issues such as fear, envy, jealousy, and low self-worth) or to put it plain, I was simply imprisoned in the "bondage of self."

The main idea behind this factor is to become willing to allow the Creator to help you when practicing spiritual principles to overcome your disturbances. I had to break through patterns of denial and come to the realization that the thinking I was working with could not change my situation. I had to change my "will" and practice what the Word says, take directions from other principle-driven people. I had to feel the pain of change by breaking my pride, and believe me, it is painful to smash your pride.

Sometimes our inner beliefs are so deeply rooted that it takes serious consequences to humble you enough to become willing to accept direction and take actions that will bring about sustained changes in your life. The meter that will tell you if there is some form of pride, self-will, or fear operating in you is any level of restlessness, irritability, and discontentment (RID).

Proverbs 3:5–Trust in the Lord with all your heart, and do not lean on your own understanding. In all your ways acknowledge him, and he will make straight your paths. The first point I want to make about this scripture is the word "understanding," which implies what we know and what we think we know , or simply, our perceptions of what we can see, taste, touch, hear, or smell. Too often, we as people go about life only trusting in what we feel and sense. That is why this scripture can be a hard one to swallow. As people I postulate that most of us tend to react to a feeling before we explore the truth that drives that feeling. If we lean on our own "understanding," we must be careful because we may act out of self-will and pride in a way that may make our situation worse. What I have come to discover about God is that often He will only show his power, grace, and mercy when we stop trying to make things happen or handle everything ourselves.

This is also a scripture that challenges the gift of free will and choice that our heavenly Father gave us. He knew before he made us that He would have to give us the way back to Him through His Son Jesus Christ. He knew that He would have to give His own self as a sacrifice so there would be a filter that does not see our sin if we accept the sacrifice of the brutal beatings, sufferings, and the cross He endured unto death. When I say "our sin" you can be truly clear on this one fact: our sin comes from our "own understanding," or as I call it, "stinking thinking." A mindset that is always about us, and never considers the other. I have learned that God's sense sometimes makes no sense to us, but our sense is nonsense if it is out of His will.

Acknowledging the Creator in all ways simply means practicing humility, gratitude, and faith. When we practice spiritual principles, we must understand that "actions" are the only way to see principles play out and have any real meaning. For example, how do you "see" faith and honesty? These spiritual principles are only concepts that cannot be seen unless there are actions that display the full manifestation of the principle. Since we are spiritual beings, our true growth comes from within, and is expressed through our flesh by words and actions. When we practice spiritual principles to change our way of thinking and behaving, most often the results will be in line with what our Creator wants from us.

When I speak of humility, I am talking about being wise enough to know that with His help we can live in line with what He expects from us. Gratitude is living and accepting Him with joy even when things do not go how we want. We will always have something to be grateful for if we simply look around us.

One of the hardest things for me to do in my past life was to find gratitude while I was being driven by my unconscious fears. Because I wanted things my way or the way I thought was best for me, I didn't realize my ego was already distorted because I thought I needed people to validate me. Through my change I realized that I am loved because God created me, and that is validation enough, something to always be grateful for.

» Are you guided by the Creator? If so, how does that manifest in your behaviors with yourself and others, and how you engage with life? (Give some examples.)

_____

_____

_____

_____

_____

_____

_____

_____

_____

_____

_____

_____

_____

_____

_____

_____

_____

_____

_____

_____

_____

_____

_____

_____

_____

_____

» Are you the only Authority in your life and if so, how does that give you hope, treat others, and treat yourself? Do you allow others to help you? (Give examples.)

_____

_____

_____

_____

_____

_____

_____

_____

_____

_____

_____

_____

_____

_____

_____

_____

_____

_____

_____

_____

_____

_____

_____

_____

_____

_____

» What does spirituality mean to you? How does it help you treat yourself and others, and live your life? What is the difference between spirituality and religion?

_____

_____

_____

_____

_____

_____

_____

_____

_____

_____

_____

_____

_____

_____

_____

_____

_____

_____

_____

_____

_____

_____

_____

_____

_____

_____

_____

_____

Chapter Two
POWER OF PRINCIPLES

This second factor is especially important and vital. Each factor from this point forward will take your fullest intention to grasp the concept and practice being a principle driven person to make changes in your life. Our feelings are often so strong and embedded in our subconscious that we simply cannot break the habit of acting solely on what we feel. If your intention is to have relationships that are enduring and loving and a life that is whole and useful, you must make decisions and act on behaviors that are driven by principles. Most often divine intervention is needed to empower you to live out your human development.

Even if you find empowerment in the motivation of others, you still have to smash your ego and be willing to take actions that may or may not make sense in your current mindset. For example, let us look at *Matthew 5:44*, when Jesus Himself says *"to love your enemies and pray for those who persecute you."* Okay, now let's get real here. Easier said than done, right? Most often our human tendency is to get revenge, or at the very least hold resentment or anger towards others who have hurt us. However the principles of courage, faith, brotherly love, perseverance, and service simply do not subscribe to our feelings. The principle of honesty might have to come into play to ask the Creator to please help you, because you simply do not have the human strength to pull of what Jesus is saying.

In my book *Faith to Freedom: From Dumpster to Doctor*, I discussed how I learned that in my past life, my feelings dominated by behaviors. If I even perceived that I was being rejected or criticized, my tendency to mitigate those feelings would be to get defensive, seek approval, and most assuredly manipulate the situation in some way to quiet my inner stress. Today I pray before taking on projects, trying new ideas, reading books, meeting people, and even when I might be in the midst of something I should be avoiding that could pull me into the sin of it all. My feelings have power and so do yours. No one gave us a manual, and no school teaches us as children and adolescents a curriculum on how to cope. We are often just told, "do not do this," or "do not do that."

I cannot say that I practice regular attendance at Twelve Step meetings despite being a former addict, due to my belief in the scripture *John 8:36*, which says, *"so if the Son sets you free you will be free indeed."* My spiritual development is ongoing, and sustained by attending the church of my choice, deepening my faith in Christ, and listening to and learning from others, including pastors and leaders I respect. For me personally, I had to learn to develop my unique relationship with the Creator, and ask Him to help me.

What I discovered and believe wholeheartedly is that "love" must be the taproot of my beliefs, the guiding principle I must accept from my Creator, if I am to represent what real recovery is and who the Creator is. Love is often misinterpreted, reduced to just being a "feeling." In fact, love is the strongest principle of all. Love is action. When you love someone, you may feel joy or happiness, but what about when times get rough, or when you do not agree with the person you say you love? What about when you are feeling discontented with the person you say you love, and trust me, you will not always feel total joy and happiness with the person you love. However, if you truly love someone you will do what is in their best interest, even when your feelings are not joyful or happy.

According to *1 Corinthians 13, "Love is patient, love is kind. It does not envy, it does not boast, it is not proud. It is not rude, it is not self-seeking, it is not easily angered, it keeps no record of wrongs. Love does not delight in evil but rejoices with the truth [...] And now these three remain: faith, hope, and love."* This scripture makes one thing clear to me, and that is without God, who is the source of all love, our human attempts to show genuine love are precarious at best.

When I got freed from crack cocaine, my faith told me that I never had to say I am an "addict," something that is often stated when attending Twelve Step meetings. I personally believe words are powerful. I am not delusional nor a fool to think that I can go back to smoking crack and will never forget the horrific experiences I went through, that I described in my book *Faith to Freedom.* I am not suggesting that the Twelve Step process is not for you or anyone else suffering from addiction and self-destructive thinking, because all addicts and people who have negative thinking patterns suffer from the bondage of self.

The addiction itself is simply the symptom, it is the way the addict has learned to mitigate their pain. I believe that spiritual development and connection to the Creator of this world can be developed many other ways, such as attending church, reading the Bible and living out its tenets, and listening to and learning from other principle-driven and spiritually-guided people who understand the power of love.

In my journey to change my life, I most assuredly practiced principles with the help of a mentor. I needed guidance to find the solutions to my problems, which I might add, always began and ended with me. I was able to experience the full process of change due to practicing principles and not acting on feelings alone. In truth, the principles outlined in the Twelve Step program are universal principles of most faiths. In the *Twelve and Twelve*, a book used in the Twelve Step process, it states that the ideas behind the steps are a group or principles, and if practiced as a way of life they will expel the obsession that the addict is dealing with, and help them to live happily and more whole.

Just to reiterate why we refer to them as spiritual principles; you cannot see a principle without action, however you can realize the effect of spiritual principles after witnessing actions that represent them. In other words, principles cannot be seen unless you are taking action to bring that principle into fruition. For example, deciding to have faith in something does not mean you have faith. If you do not act to show that you are walking in faith, then faith itself is merely a concept or idea. Faith must have a form of expression, if faith is to be seen.

I have come to learn that many people say they have faith, however there is nothing in their actions to prove that they are living that principle. Another example, when someone says they believe in God, Buddha, Allah, or some other, that does not necessarily mean they have faith, if their behaviors are not showing that they believe in the tenets of that religion. Just because someone prays or attends religious gatherings does not mean they have faith. Yes, there is an act of faith to show up and pray, however if their behaviors are not changing based on what they say they believe in, then they are not really living out the principle of faith.

Your conscious and unconscious thinking and your perception have the power to induce feelings, and feelings drive behavior. Perception can be blinding and debilitating because we each have our own. You must get to know yourself from deep within. Develop insight into what your self-talk is and practice exploring the truth behind what you are feeling.

Principles don't subscribe to human emotions and feelings. Principles are truths, they are what they are. Just because you do not *feel* like doing something does not mean you should not do it, and just because you *feel* like doing something does not mean you should do it. If you execute and organize around principles, you can become more independently minded, which can give you the potential to have more healthy interdependent relationships with others and reach goals in your life.

During the early course of my life, I was a victim to my own feelings. I reacted to whatever I felt instead of responding to the reality of situations or events. My ego-motivated choices often produced stumbling blocks and pitfalls. However, if you make choices based on being true to yourself and on principle—not the "don't you know who I think I am" false self—you are creating chances to grow.

Every choice that shows you have respect for yourself and others will bring you that much closer to being who you are meant to be in the universe. When fear or other negative emotions drive our decisions and behaviors, we invariably stay in a state of disillusion, and will always experience some form of hurt, anger, disappointment, or resentment, and more than likely hurt others.

Proverbs 28:26–Whoever trusts in his own mind is a fool, but he who walks in wisdom will be delivered. When I explored and shared my past life with you in my book *Faith to Freedom*, I discussed how I was often driven by a fear of rejection; I constantly sought the approval of others and was always people-pleasing. Now, I need you to think about that. If I was currently operating in that state of mind there is no way I could have accomplished a sense of peace and serenity with my life. There is no way I could trust and be vulnerable to explore myself and admit my wrongs to others, and I most assuredly would have quit school because of the many sacrifices it took me to avoid bad influences and control my spending habits, so I could pay for school and get all my debts paid.

If I continued taking actions based on what I was feeling, I would simply get the same results over and over, a continued dissatisfaction with life due to an unconscious faulty belief system. I would stay disappointed because I would not be happy within. Principles have outcomes that do not change, but feelings will always change. For example, if I am honest about something, I never have to remember what I said or have done. The principle of honesty stays the same. However, if I continue to manipulate or deceive, time may pass and I may forget what I said or have done. Another example, the principle of faith and courage helped me to go to school even when my feelings of uncertainty and fear kept me uncomfortable. I simply kept studying, kept reading, kept asking for help, and did all that was assigned to me. At the end of the day, the principles of faith, courage, willingness, perseverance, and hope were able to have their truest expression in my life, because I refused to give in to my feelings and was able to accomplish some of my goals.

The principles I am alluding to are ones like Honesty, Hope, Integrity, Trust, Willingness, Restitution, Humility, Brotherhood, Perseverance, Service, Patience, Tolerance and Forgiveness, to name a few. These principles and more will surely test and challenge your feelings, especially in difficult times. When I wrote this book, it was not my intention to tell you to believe what I believe. However, I challenge you to practice any of these principles in times of trouble and let honesty be the foundation principle. I promise you that your outcomes will be more enduring and sustained.

At the end of my book *Faith to Freedom*, I wrote a ten-step coping strategy that challenges your feelings in times of struggle when you are restless, irritable, and discontented. If you can be honest with yourself in this process, I can almost guarantee there will be a solution. The problem might be your inability to accept the solution, based on what you are feeling, however the principles will not change.

Galatians 5:22-23–But the fruit of the Spirit is love, joy, peace, patience, kindness, goodness, faithfulness, gentleness, self-control; against such things there is no law. This scripture makes it clear that nothing in this universe will change the outcome of practicing principles. However principles can change your outcome and situations.

When we act solely on our feelings, as I learned was something that I often did in my past life, we end up disappointed, hurt, resentful, and angry. *Proverbs 25:28, "A man without self-control is like a city broken into and left without walls."* Our lifeline and power from the Creator come to us by practicing principles (i.e., the fruits of His Spirit) when we are making decisions, in communication with others, or making changes in our lives. Principles are His guiding tools—if we take action to live them out—for us to live useful, purposeful, and whole.

Lastly and especially important, is to seek the counsel and guidance of others who are purpose and principle driven. If you are trying to change self-destructive behaviors, repair a relationship, break a bad habit, or simply change your life for the better, it is essential to practice the principle of hope by associating with like-minded people. Practice the principles of humility and trust to allow yourself to be vulnerable enough to get the help you need. We cannot go it alone.

» Do you make most of your decisions based on feelings and emotions? If so, what usually happens?

_____

_____

_____

_____

_____

_____

_____

_____

_____

_____

_____

_____

_____

_____

_____

_____

_____

_____

_____

_____

_____

_____

_____

_____

» Why do you think honesty, humility, and courage are important principles to practice? How can they help you make correct decisions in all areas of your life? How could these principles be uncomfortable to practice?

_____

_____

_____

_____

_____

_____

_____

_____

_____

_____

_____

_____

_____

_____

_____

_____

_____

_____

_____

_____

_____

_____

_____

_____

_____

_____

_____

Chapter Three
UNCOVER AND DISCOVER "YOU"

The process of changing your thinking and behavior is not a linear or rigid process, however it is wise to have counseling or simply be in the counsel of others. People often see us in ways we do not see ourselves. We must remember that our internal world, our subconscious beliefs and perceptions can easily be distorted. We must also understand the powerful impact that culture has in forming our beliefs. Culture is a unique factor of human development that drives us all through life.

It would be wise to seek a professional therapist, counselor, or psychologist in most cases if you want to make significant changes by exploring how you developed your thinking patterns, and how you have come to view yourself and the world around you. However, having a friend, pastor, spiritual advisor, or other person you can trust to talk to about your thoughts and feelings is surely a good start. In the process of personal change, you must consider that there are various methods and strategies one could use to help them make the necessary paradigm shifts that will help them change behaviors. Learning to accept your "authentic" self can be very scary and seem like traveling unchartered waters.

For example, our culture is one of the strongest forces that shapes our beliefs. Culture is a tool of the mind. It is an individual's way of seeing and interacting in the world. It encompasses one's value system, beliefs, and perception of the world around them. Race, socio-economic class, gender, sexual orientation, ability, geographic location, age, religion, and language all impact the formation of culture. The way in which an individual is socialized within their family and community around race, class, religion, and language will impact the formation of their values and beliefs, which then becomes their culture.

Culture is fluid; it is not a static entity which one takes out of a box on occasions. It is with us daily. The manifestations of our culture are seen in the ways we carry out our daily activities—anything from washing a dish, to eating a particular-food, to having specific styles of communication. The ways in which we approach and implement our daily activities will demonstrate our cultural upbringing. Culture is an internal process, it is formulated within and through the interactions of many facets which impact our lives. The manifestation of culture happens externally on a regular basis. This means that all of us have a culture, and we are continually living in the moment of our culture, our tool of the mind.

According to Steven Covey's book, *The Seven Principles of Highly Effective People*, the place to begin building any relationship is inside ourselves. As we become independent—proactive, centered in correct principles, value-driven, and able to organize our life with integrity—we can then choose to become interdependent, capable of building rich, enduring, and productive relationships with other people.

Romans 12:3–For by the grace given to me I say to everyone among you not to think of himself more highly than he ought to think, but to think with sober judgment, each according to the measure of faith that God has assigned.

In my book *Faith To Freedom: From Dumpster To Doctor*, I discussed that in my past life I operated on a fear-driven belief system rooted in a selfish pursuit of happiness, or what I perceived happiness to be (e.g., more money, bigger car, lots of jewelry, a better lover, nice clothes, being a superstar known by everyone). My internal beliefs were driving me to feel insecure, unworthy, and fearful, most often because of being rejected or not being accepted. My judgment no doubt was clouded in distorted faulty beliefs, while my instincts for emotional security also operated. This was an unknown and subconscious dilemma for me. Fear, like any other negative emotion, has one purpose and that is to serve its own agenda. Negative emotions can only be eradicated or mitigated by principles that are grounded in truth.

During my journey to have a more productive, useful, and purposeful life, it became essential that I practice enough humility, integrity, courage, and open-mindedness to accept help from other purpose-driven people who would only tell me the truth. I needed others to help me explore the deeper meaning of my self-imposed crises, even if it meant I had to admit that I was selfish and self-centered.

Proverbs 27:17—Iron sharpens iron, and one man sharpens another. As stated above, the Word makes it clear that if I am to be a better me, or a more purposeful and useful me, I must allow others to give me direction that will bring about correction. We need to be able to take feedback and constructive criticism because sometimes people see us very differently than we see ourselves.

When I look back, I can see this as a truth. When I charmed others or acted in kindness to get my way and then things did *not* go my way, the "other me" would show up in my attitude change, which led to others getting hurt in some way. My motives were often unknown to me and had to be explored. If you are serious about making changes in your life that will show love to others and allow God to direct you, you will want to ensure that the root of your thinking is not driven by selfish pride.

1 Corinthians 11:28—Let a person examine himself, then, and so eat of the bread and drink of the cup.

During my past life I had the gifts of being a good leader and having a kind heart for people, however those gifts could not truly manifest. Selfishness, self-centeredness, and fear dominated me. I was stagnating in isolation unable to express my innermost feelings in fear of rejection and making myself vulnerable to others. Even my resentment towards others who used or abused me as a child when I did nothing to deserve it, became a block preventing me from loving and accepting myself.

When we get hurt, we are surely justified to be angry, especially when we were innocent children. When we become adults our resentments that are unforgiven and unresolved, have the power to rob us of our freedom. Unfortunately, no matter how bad we have been hurt, forgiveness is the only way out and the only way to break stagnation and isolation. If we continue to carry the baggage of the past and it continues to weigh us down, how can we truly serve and help others? Whenever we carry around the guilt and shame from people we have harmed or who have harmed us, it stunts our growth as people. All areas of our lives are affected, especially our self-esteem. The focus stayed on my resentments, people I harmed, my sexual misconduct, and the fears.

The process I used while working with a mentor and

other principle-driven people was very instrumental in me identifying the part I played in my internal mess. When I became trusting enough to share my innermost pain, fears, and regrets, the self-centered part of me that kept blaming others and being a victim inadvertently broke through isolation and through being vulnerable, felt a sense of connection with the world.

I was able to smash my fear-driven ego and finally do away with being fake and a constant people-pleaser, seeking validation. I developed a profound sense of being my most honest self. I discovered my liabilities and my assets and forgave myself through action and doing things that were loving and nurturing. I stopped manipulating to get my needs met and did my best to correct my mistakes.

Matthew 7:3-5–Why do you see the speck that is in your brother's eye, but do not notice the log that is in your own eye? Or how can you say to your brother, 'Let me take the speck out of your eye,' when there is the log in your own eye? You hypocrite, first take the log out of your own eye, and then you will see clearly to take the speck out of your brother's eye. This scripture is profound, yet so simple and true. The practice of introspection, examining myself and the decisions I have made throughout my life, has also enhanced my gift of empathy. Knowing your authentic self will invariably give you some degree of empathy, tolerance, and love towards others.

» Why is it important to practice courage, integrity, and trust to discover your true self?

_____

_____

_____

_____

_____

_____

_____

_____

_____

_____

_____

_____

_____

_____

_____

_____

_____

_____

_____

_____

_____

_____

_____

_____

_____

» Why is it important to know who you really are? How does that help you live a more useful and productive life?

_____

_____

_____

_____

_____

_____

_____

_____

_____

_____

_____

_____

_____

_____

_____

_____

_____

_____

_____

_____

_____

_____

_____

_____

_____

_____

Chapter Four
FORGIVENESS

Let this key factor be an ongoing one. Some people will never forgive you or themselves; they are simply incapable of being honest enough with themselves enough to practice this principle. We all want to be forgiven in our own lives, we have all made mistakes and may have hurt others. People who refuse to forgive past transgressions or at the very least become willing to forgive, give themselves the excuse to blame, point the finger, and play God.

Someone else's willingness to forgive you or not forgive you is God's business. Simply clean your side of the street with a true and contrite heart that takes full responsibility. The kind of responsibility where you experience remorse and regret for wrongs you have done. False pride in any form is self-destructive thinking. Humility is key.

For example, in my past life when I was using drugs there was one occasion where I stole one thousand dollars from a female acquaintance. In my travels being clean from drugs and walking in my new life, I saw this person standing on the stairs of my daughter's school, where I was going to pick her up. While sitting in my car contemplating how I was going to approach her to make the amends she deserved and that I knew I had to make, it dawned on me to also give her back the money I had stolen from her.

Well it just so happened that I had exactly one thousand and fifty dollars in my bank, and bills that were due. I said a quiet prayer and felt it in my spirit to simply be obedient to the principles of faith, courage, brotherly love, and justice, and to go to her to make the amends. As the story goes, I approached her and asked if she could please forgive me for lying to her, being selfish, and stealing her money while I was on drugs. I also apologized for perpetrating a fraud and living a double life by trying to hide my addiction, all the while having selfish motives to get what I wanted from her. She replied very angrily, saying loudly, and I quote, "Take your crackhead money and shove it up your ass, and get the f…k out of my face."

At that very moment my old fear-driven ego tried to creep in and say something in retaliation, however the spirit overwhelmed me with humility to simply say, "I understand and acknowledge your hurt and pain, and respect your decision for me to get out of your face."

I walked into the building to get my daughter feeling low and broken. It never dawned on me that I had hurt her more than just stealing from her. I felt the pain from her response, that she may have developed feelings for me in the past and my manipulations had deeply wounded her. After I picked up my daughter, I said a quiet prayer and immediately I received the revelation, "it was good you took the actions you took, and you were also able to keep your money to pay your bills." What also dawned on me is that if I ever see her again, she could not accuse me of not trying to make right my wrongs, and I can walk with dignity and self-respect.

It is easy to understand in our human limitations why people who have been hurt will not forgive. However, we must consider this factor. When you hurt someone (and trust me, you have) or if you leave a stain of resentment in someone's heart based on something you did in your human weakness, think about how you desire their forgiveness. More importantly, think about when you hit your knees and pray, and ask the Creator to please forgive you and give you another chance. Think about someone you love like your children, parents, or any other loved ones that you may have hurt, whether it was intentional or unintentional. I know you want their forgiveness.

Matthew 5:44—but I say you, love your enemy, pray for those who persecute you. In this scripture, Jesus gives us a profound direction to forgive and pray for others, even when they hurt you. In our selfish human nature this command by Christ makes no sense, especially when many of us have been wounded in our lives, often by our own family members. During my childhood I felt unsafe, afraid, and often persecuted by my stepfather. However, this scripture and those who practice true forgiveness have guided me to practice praying for him and all others I have been hurt by or who I perceived to have hurt me.

We are all selfish by nature to some degree, others perhaps moreso than their fellow. However, the principle of love and my desire to change my life gave me the courage to practice forgiveness. When I speak about needing love and courage to practice forgiveness, I mean that I had to examine why it was so hard to forgive. I discovered that living in fear and being a victim was easier because it gave me an excuse to blame others for my failures or my inability to strive for more. I realized that it takes courage to forgive because my ego and selfish nature would not accept the limitations of others.

I was once directed by a mentor to get on my knees every night for two weeks and pray for every good thing that I wanted for myself for any person who I feel hurt me in my life and to start with my parents or primary caretakers, whether they were alive or not. Since my desire for change was stronger than my desire to stay in a hopeless victim state of mind, I took his direction. To my surprise my prayers went from being precarious in nature to very sincere. I prayed that my dad was in heaven enjoying God's love's and paradise.

I asked God to forgive me for not forgiving his human limitations as well as my own. I stopped questioning how He allowed things to happen to me, to shape me. I prayed fervently for my mother, that God would bring joy, peace, love, and happiness to her life, and that she would live the rest of her days feeling overwhelmed with love. After praying sincerely and asking God to give me the willingness to let go of all resentments I held against others, because some of them were very hard to let go of, I discovered that I became free from the hurt of my past.

Now I give my mother many hugs, tell her how much I love her, and give her money every month, even though she does not need it. I am free from all the resentments of my past. My life started to progress and simply get better. It was as if a flow of divine energy started to give me power to achieve, and blessings started to flow.

It is my opinion that one day you will have to answer to the Creator and consider that you were not even willing to forgive your brother or sister who you can see. Yet you ask the Creator who you cannot see, to forgive you for something you have done. Pain that others may have caused you can leave deep wounds and feel impossible to forgive, however I believe we must at least consider forgiving, so you can heal and move on.

Forgiveness is for you and making amends to those you hurt acknowledges them and hopefully gives them more opportunity to be willing to forgive others they may have hurt. My hope is that you at least become willing to forgive, even if at first you feel you cannot. Willingness is like a key that will give you the potential to at least "unlock the door" to the idea of forgiveness.

I found that forgiveness, despite sometimes seeming impossible, especially in cases of severe trauma, will shed light on your own limitations. Your willingness to consider forgiveness will help you realize how throughout your life, you have caused at the very least some emotional or mental pain to others, even if it was unintentional.

This key factor of forgiveness could be considered "surgery on the soul." Instead of repressing your hurt and anger, forgiveness releases the cancer of resentment, and brings freedom to your mind. Today I have completely and totally forgiven everyone who physically, emotionally, spiritually, or mentally hurt me, including myself.

I love them all as well as myself, and I recognize that just like me, they have human limitations and weaknesses. Yes, some past pain, especially childhood trauma when the victim has no power to defend themselves can seem impossible to forgive. However the principle of forgiveness does not subscribe to human emotions, and our Father in Heaven made it clear that forgiveness is what He desires from us. Please recognize that forgiving others is for you and will empower you and set you free.

When we get hurt, we are surely justified to be angry, especially when we were innocent children. When become adults, our unforgiven and unresolved resentments have the power to rob us of our ability to be free. Unfortunately, no matter how bad we have been hurt in the past or present, forgiveness is the only way out and the only way to break stagnation and isolation. If we continue to carry the baggage of the past and let it weigh us down, how can we truly serve and help others? When we refuse to forgive and let others know we have forgiven them, then pride is our master. Pride cuts us off from the sunlight of the spirit because pride is selfish and serves no one except itself.

» How do you know you have forgiven yourself and why do you need to forgive yourself?

_____
_____
_____
_____
_____
_____
_____
_____
_____
_____
_____
_____
_____
_____
_____
_____
_____
_____
_____
_____
_____
_____
_____
_____
_____
_____

» Why is it important to forgive others? How will that improve your life to be more productive and transformative?

_____

_____

_____

_____

_____

_____

_____

_____

_____

_____

_____

_____

_____

_____

_____

_____

_____

_____

_____

_____

_____

_____

_____

_____

_____

Chapter Five
NURTURE YOUR PHYSICAL SELF

Eat healthy consistently and indulge as a treat. A healthy balance of essential macro-nutrients such as carbohydrates, protein, and "good" lipids (i.e., fats), water, and multivitamins can give the body and mind the highest potential to perform. Yes, our bodies will eventually deteriorate, but you must do what you can to live your best life today. It is pleasing to God when we take care of our health because we can better serve him. Your body is a temple! Focus on getting proper rest. The body needs to heal, and healing is done properly when you are resting. Exercise modestly, after all the body will perform if we consistently use it.

Muscles must be used, or they will become weak and start to atrophy. Exercise will help give you endurance and promote weight management. Your body and how you feel about it will invariably affect your mind and spirit. You only have this body while you are here, alive on Earth. Take care of it, honor it, and nurture it. Do not obsess on it and do not obsess on vanity. Love who you are and be who you are.

When I was an athlete during my adolescent years, I realized even then how running kept me feeling energetic and gave me a sense of positive self-esteem even while I struggled with feelings of unworthiness. Somehow exercise gave me hope that if I kept my physical health, I could make it.

During my years of drug use, when I had moments of abstinence, I would often work out and do things good for my body to counter what I knew was bad for me. Today, practicing consistent and moderate exercises continues to give me a healthy sense of self.

Being a man of fifty-seven years of age at the time of writing this book, I cannot see myself not exercising and just sitting around. Although age is a factor and time is getting short, I would rather have the best health and best life before I leave this earth rather than feel lethargic and not be useful in the service of others. No matter what your age is, being purposeful and intentional to nurture your health and take care of the only body you have gives honor to the Creator who made you. Part of the physical nurturing process is to get regular checkups from a medical doctor and stay proactive and responsible for both your physical and mental health.

Yes, there might be struggles with weight; yes, there might be struggles with physical limitations; however, if there is something you can do to promote a healthier physical state it is your duty and responsibility to take care of what you do have. *1 Corinthian 6:19-20* states, *"do you not know that your body is a temple of the Holy Spirit within you, whom you have from God? You are not your own, for you were bought with a price. So, glorify God in your body."* In this scripture, Paul makes it clear that taking care of your physical health brings glory to God. When Paul refers to your body not being your own, He makes it clear you did not make or create yourself. When you take care of yourself, you are also showing discipline and gratitude to the Creator because he made you and made an extreme sacrifice for you.

When I talk about taking care of yourself, I am not speaking from the idea of false pride or vanity. We are so often bombarded with propaganda from the media, such as television and magazines, that our motives for physical health can easily become driven more by appearance and your perception of what you "should" look like. The reason I consider this factor important is simple: when you feel better about your image, your health, and you have energy to work and enjoy healthy recreation, it promotes self-esteem and good mental health.

Ecclesiastes 1:8 states, *"Everything is so weary and tiresome! No matter how much we see, we are never satisfied. No matter how much we hear, we are not content."* This scripture reveals the importance of simply keeping balance in your life, and to be mindful that being principle driven (as discussed in Chapter Two) will help reduce the discontentment in life that is so easy to experience. Our physical bodies are just as important as our mental and spiritual wellbeing, because each one is connected. Yes, we will ultimately leave these bodies, but we are living in them now. So be intentional to honor and respect the "temple" you reside in for the time you have left here on Earth.

Below are important key points for maintaining your physical health:

Nutrients

- Dietary guidelines recommend that you consume 45-65% of your calories from carbohydrates, 10-35% from protein, and 20-35% calories from fat (i.e., good fats)
- Drink plenty of water (about eight glasses a day). Drinking water helps maintain your balance of body fluids. The body is composed of about 60% water. The functions of these bodily fluids include digestion, absorption, circula-

tion, creation of saliva, transport of nutrients, and maintenance of body temperature.

- Your body uses water in all its cells and organs. Because your body loses water through breathing, sweating, and digestion, it is important to rehydrate by drinking fluids and eating foods that contain water, like fruits and vegetables.

Sleep and rest
- promote healthy cognitive function
- promotes healthy healing of internal functions within the body, including muscle repair, fat burning, and brain function
- feelings of well-being
- energy and vitality
- improved mood

Exercise
- Increase muscle endurance
- Releases natural endorphins (i.e., chemicals that trigger positive feelings like morphine)
- Increase cardio-respiratory functioning
- Helps control weight management, including weight loss
- Raising the resting metabolic rate (Basal Metabolic Rate). The body's generation of heat is known as thermogenesis and it can be measured to determine the amount of energy expended. BMR generally decreases with age and with a decrease in lean body mass (i.e., muscle). So it is even more important to exercise as you get older, to give your body the best opportunity to perform.
- Regular exercise can have a profoundly positive impact on depression, anxiety, attention deficit hyperactivity disorder, and more. It also relieves stress, improves memory,

helps you sleep better, and boosts your overall mood. And you do not have to be a fitness fanatic to reap the benefits.

Multivitamins

- Take a multivitamin daily. A multivitamin is like an insurance policy, a daily guarantee to ensure your body gets the vitamins and mineral it needs, especially because it could be difficult to get all the food groups and the proper balance of nutrients on a daily basis. As you get older, your nutritional needs increase. At the same time, it gets harder to for the body to absorb nutrients.

As I started the process of making sustained changes in my life, I was able to appreciate the important knowledge I received about my physical health when I became a personal fitness trainer and attended college. As we age, this factor must be especially important to practice on a consistent basis, to give yourself the best chance to fulfill and live out your life in the best way possible.

No matter how much money or material success you attain, no matter how spiritual you become (and you cannot be too spiritual if you do not honor your temple), your happiness with self will be precarious at best. I might remind you as well that self-destructive thinking can also produce poor eating habits, which can lead to obesity, lethargy, and procrastination, especially if you eat to compensate for unresolved internal stress. Do not "live to eat," but eat to live. Stinking thinking drives people to eat unhealthily and avoid their responsibility to maintain good physical health.

» How are you mindful to take care of your physical health?
Give 3 examples below:

_____

_____

_____

_____

_____

_____

_____

_____

_____

_____

_____

_____

_____

_____

_____

_____

_____

_____

_____

_____

_____

_____

_____

_____

_____

_____

» How does your physical health improve your mind, spirit, and relationships to others? Give examples of all three:

_____
_____
_____
_____
_____
_____
_____
_____
_____
_____
_____
_____
_____
_____
_____
_____
_____
_____
_____
_____
_____
_____
_____
_____
_____

Chapter Six
MONEY ON PURPOSE

Get help understanding money and establishing and keeping good credit. It is an unfortunate reality that we need money to survive this world we live in and take care of our basic needs. If we are going to sustain our lives, we must be intentional to think about why, when, and where, we spend money. If *stinking thinking* such as "I *need* this to be liked or found worthy" drives your behaviors to get money, more often than not you will never be satisfied. Money will have power over you because your inner unconscious thoughts are faulty. There is no way around this factor. The system of the world operates under the premise of product, goods, and services that cost. Most of the products and services are simply to sustain our life, such as food, water, shelter, and clothing. The hope is to be financially free, yet the reality is there is only a small percentage of rich and wealthy people in the world that do not have to borrow money or need help as most of the middle and lower economic classes do.

Since this is the reality of our existence, then we must examine our thoughts about money. When I talked about credit worthiness, I am talking about character that includes integrity, discipline, reliability, and honesty. You do not need to be perfect to pay money back. Yes, sometimes in life things happen that disrupt our ability to pay debt. However, if you are having a hard time meeting financial deadlines, it is important to be proactive and responsible and not just ignore your obligations. Having a good name is essential. Keep your word if you borrow money and if you can't pay it back as promised, be humble enough to take responsibility. Inform who you are obligated to pay back what your plan to pay them back is, and be sure to honor your obligations and pay back the money you owe.

Consider and act on our first key factor. Give to God first; help others such as the poor, the sick, the children, or causes that help mankind. Give to your church, especially if they are helping other causes. When you give from your heart, the concept of reaping what you sow comes to fruition. Giving also heals and builds your spirit, and says a lot about what you think and care about. It is a real sign of healthy thinking, because you understand the importance of consideration for others.

Proverbs 14:31—Whoever oppresses the poor shows contempt for their Maker, but whoever is kind to the needy honors God. This scripture warns us against focusing too much on the rules of tithing without paying attention to the more important things like justice, mercy, and faithfulness. Yes, we should tithe, but we should not leave undone the more important things *(Matthew 23:23)*. Often you hear pastors preach about tithing, and rightfully so, however there are many who preach tithing while the church is doing nothing outside of its four walls. This will bring debate, however it is my opinion that if we are to help the church increase its ministry to share the gospel of love, then the church body must give to causes that help those who are poor, hungry, sick, and downtrodden. You decide.

For the many years I was addicted to drugs, my debts got bigger and my credit was nonexistent. As far as finances go, I was ignorant and very unwise. Most often my ego and my feelings about what I thought I needed to give a false impression of being someone successful became impossible to live up to. On my journey of recovery, I had to research via the internet, literature, certified public accountants, business professionals, bankers, insurance brokers, and agents, how to establish excellent credit, invest money, build my financial status, and develop long-term financial plans, which subsequently built character in me.

I wrote all my creditors and started to pay back a little at a time. I paid my debts despite my egotistical desires (stinking thinking) to please myself. I was told that rebuilding my "good name" and credit worthiness would take time, and if I wanted to build my financial profile I had to be courageous and faithful to think about others such as my family and things bigger than myself, if I wanted to stay motivated to build a financial profile. Money had to have purpose and legacy.

I learned the importance of establishing a rapport with bankers, financial planners, insurance brokers, and businessmen and women who could help me understand and create a financial plan that would take care of my family, my retirement needs, and create some sort of legacy for my future generation. What I learned is that the most profound act of love is to plan to leave a legacy and help for my wife, my children, and their children. This way of thinking motivated me to develop the attitude to become creative and disciplined in my finances. The beautiful thing about being disciplined in your finances is that it will also create opportunities to give you some of the things you like in life, such as cars, homes, vacations, and other material possessions that bring comfort and enjoyment. There is nothing wrong with enjoying some of the finer things in life, if those things do not become idols or extensions of delusional thinking. For example, buying a new car to impress others to feed your ego (which I might add will only be temporary) is total stinking thinking and will keep you chasing money for the wrong reasons. If you are not happy or content with yourself, no material possession will fix you.

Becoming an owner of a home, being debt free, having life insurance, being able to pay your bills, and being able to help family and causes bigger that yourself is rewarding and will add years to your life. The love of money is sinful when we use it for selfish purposes. When we trust money rather than God to solve our problems, we are surely in stinking thinking. Those who pursue its empty promises will one day discover that they have nothing if they are spiritually bankrupt. If you are capable, consider investing, or at the very least save some money. Most importantly, take what finances you do have and discuss with others as I have listed above, how to spend it wisely, save it, budget it to grow, gain true understanding of your finances in the context of your earnings, and have something to assure you will survive rough times.

Protect your legacy and family by obtaining insurance and try to leave something for your children and grandchildren. Seek, pray, and work for generational wealth. Think bigger than yourself when it pertains to money. This idea will surely give you inspiration, purpose, and vision, and drive you to work harder and explore ways to create finances that not only bless you but bless others.

Acts 20:35–In all things I have shown you that by working hard in this way we must help the weak and remember the words of the

Lord Jesus, how he himself said, "It is more blessed to give than to receive." When I look back on my life, I realize that I already had a heart to give, however it was hard to be true to my heart because I was profoundly driven by fear to appear as someone I was not. My heart was compromised by my inability to think of others while in the bondage of self and my need to impress others for validation, especially women. So my idea of money and possessions in the past were distorted and placed in the wrong order. When I was delivered from addiction, I still had to unlearn the faulty beliefs about myself and the need for validation which had the power to drive me to spend money recklessly and unwisely.

Acts 8:20–But Peter said unto him, thy money perishes with thee, because thou hast thought that the gift of God may be purchased with money. In this scripture, Peter makes it clear that if we are to serve and show love to others, we must use our money to bring glory to God and not ourselves. It is ok to have money, but let money have a purpose that is bigger than you. Discipline in our finance often means sacrifice, which will sometimes challenge what we feel we need or ought to have.

Ecclesiastes 11:1-6–Give generously, for your gifts will return to you later. Divided your gifts among many, for you do not know what risk might lie ahead. When clouds are heavy, the rain comes down. When tree falls, whether south or north, there it lies. If you wait for perfect conditions, you will never get anything done. God's ways are as hard to discern as the pathways of the wind, and as mysterious as a tiny baby being formed in a mothers' womb. Be sure to stay busy and plant a variety of crops, for you never know which will grow—perhaps they all will.

Do not worry if you are acknowledged or not, give in secret and not to show everyone. Help your family by giving them a "hand-up" and not constant "handouts." Remember some will constantly try to use you, and feel entitled to keep doing it if you are successful or kindhearted, especially family or friends.

Lastly, consider that we must all "bite the humble pie" and work hard to develop our human potential. Be sure to give to real causes, like organizations that help the sick, the poor and those involved in research and education that will bring about cures for illnesses, because it is extremely rewarding and God's will. At the end of the day, the world is bigger than us individually. This factor brings joy and a sense of purpose to my life. It reminds me that to whom much is given, much is required. I cannot take money or the things of this world with me when I die. Use money on purpose, for purpose.

» Write down ten things you do with your money. Do any of those ten things have purpose and meaning bigger than you?

» Do you have a budget? If not… why not? Do you pay your bills on time, and if not why? Is your spending attached to what you feel? Please explain so you can see your own truth.

_____

_____

_____

_____

_____

_____

_____

_____

_____

_____

_____

_____

_____

_____

_____

_____

_____

_____

_____

_____

_____

_____

_____

_____

» What is your understanding of money and how does it have purpose in your life?

Chapter Seven
"DON'T BE A HATER"

It is very easy to make assumptions about other people successes, however most often you have no clue what it took another person to become who they are or obtain what they have. I had to learn to support others' success by praying for them and acknowledging them. I had to stop measuring myself by what I perceived others had.

I learned that it is easy to envy others if you are not trying to be the best you, and especially if you are allowing fear to dominate your life. To envy and covet is futile and foolish. There was a time in my life that it was easy to covet the successes of others, or what I perceived their successes were, because I knew I could do better with my own life and I was creating my own mess.

If you focus on others or envy others' success without recognizing the principle of "sacrifice" (or what it took them to become who they are), you are simply living in a delusional state of mind. Fear is dominating your existence. We all have our paths and nothing we achieve in material value means anything if our spirits and our characters are not right.

Ecclesiastes 4: 5-6–Then I observed that most people are motivated to success by their envy of their neighbors. But this, too, is meaningless, like chasing the wind. Foolish people refuse to work and almost starve. They feel it is better to be lazy and barely survive than to work hard, especially when in the long run everything is so futile. This scripture is so meaningful because at the end of the day, you will never be happy until you tap into your own inner resources, live in your gifts, and go after your dreams based on the purpose the Creator has for you.

It might be scary, however if you do not try to overcome your fears, set goals, and work hard to realize your dreams and develop your own gifts at your own pace, envy can creep in and keep you feeling miserable and being a "hater," for lack of a better term. This factor has become so real for me after seeing how others have perceived and treated me, and hearing some of the remarks they said to me. It was so easy for me to realize their envy of me. They never asked what I experienced while I was in the process of earning my college degrees, putting in many hours of work and making sacrifices to grow no matter what I was feeling or how much fear I was experiencing. They never asked me about the many nights I sat up and cried, wanting to give up while I had another exam to study for or paper to write. And they didn't know about the many trips to the emergency room I took, thinking I was dying of a heart attack when it turned out to be anxiety.

When you start to love yourself enough to make sacrifices for the sake of growth in your life, there is ultimately a harvest that will come. As I was able to establish solid finances and obtain some material possessions such as new cars, homes, and enjoying some of the finer things that life had to offer, I encountered and still do encounter those we call "haters."

When you are focused and driven you do not have time to envy others and what they are doing, because you have your own measuring tool for what success means to you. Your validation becomes the "man in the mirror," because you know who you belong to and that the Creator is the only validation you need.

James 3:16–For where jealousy and selfish ambition exist, there will be disorder and every vile practice. For many years in my past life I experienced jealousy and envy of others who were doing well or who I perceived as a threat to me, due mostly to my insecurities, fear of failure, and fear of success, especially while under the grip of addiction.

Moreover, my drug-seeking behaviors caused so much guilt and shame in me, and affirmed my subconscious faulty belief that I was not good enough. My own inner stinking thinking produced feelings that simply kept me in a state of perpetual fear, which subsequently brought about more negative emotions such as envy and jealousy.

Fear had a way of driving me to seek the easy way out, and to continue to manipulate events to temporarily quiet my insecure feelings. For example, I would often act like someone I was not when I would go to a nightclub. My fakeness would often work for a while, when trying to get a date or sleep with a woman. However soon the "real" me, the man who was afraid, manipulative, and hooked on drugs would emerge and the women would get hurt. I knew intuitively that I was wrong and my morals were constantly compromised, however my fears and insecurities made it easy for jealousy, envy, and desiring what others had to be a constant threat to me. Deep inside, I knew I could do better with my life.

To be jealous of others is truly a waste of time and a sign of fear and lack of courage to accept yourself. These negative emotions are always driven by stinking thinking. We each have a journey. You must ask yourself, is fear preventing you from doing what you really want for yourself and making the necessary sacrifice of time, effort, money, and discipline? Can you feel comfortable being yourself despite who is around? Do you have a bad habit or some type of vice that prevents you from living out your dreams or that keeps you feeling shameful? If you envy or are jealous of others, trust me, one of those questions needs to be answered. It may be time for you to practice the courage and honesty it takes to improve your life.

When I stopped using drugs and started working as personal trainer, saving my money, paying my bills on time, attending college, and doing good for others and my family gave me a sense of positive self-esteem which became a self-perpetuating cycle of motivation and affirmation. I wanted more for myself. I was able to look at myself in the mirror and like the person I was becoming. My jealousy and envy of others started to disappear because I knew I was doing good things and being responsible for myself and others. My need for validation and approval started to go away.

When you act in ways that are nurturing and loving to yourself (i.e., doing things based on principles and not feelings) you gradually gain a sense of confidence. What others have or what they are doing becomes insignificant to you. You start to admire the gifts and talents of others and appreciate the differences between you. If you are where you are supposed to be and doing positive things to build your own life such as working hard, making sacrifices, and being focused and principle-driven, fear of the world and what other people think will gradually diminish.

Lastly, and also profoundly for me, many years ago I began intentionally and purposefully praying for people who have gained influence and financial successes in the world, such as Oprah, Obama and Michelle, Beyoncé, Tyler Perry, The Jackson Family, Whitney Houston and her family, Kobe Bryant and his family, Lebron James, Steve Harvey, Michael Jordan and a few others that I truly admire. I thank the Creator that he has allowed me to live and see gifts in them and others.

What I find compelling about the people above is their passion for their respective crafts. I am a passionate person, so it is easy to enjoy and become intrigued by the passion of others. I have come to enjoy who I am without regard to what others perceive about me. I am a gift, and so are you. However until you embrace the gift that is you, it will be hard to think positively towards others.

I strongly believe that if we first overcome our false self and become our true self, it is extremely easy to celebrate the successes and gifts that others have. We can pray for their protection, pray that they are blessed, and admire the gifts that God gave to them. I believe there is a boomerang effect that will come upon your life when you can celebrate the life and blessings of others by thinking positively about them. It might not come in the form of their influence or financial status; however, it might bring great health and blessings upon you, your children, and your family and friends.

» How does hating on others bring negative effects in every area of your life such as mind, body, spirit, and relationships? Explain. How could hating on others disrupt positive transformation in your life?

_____

_____

_____

_____

_____

_____

_____

_____

_____

_____

_____

_____

_____

_____

_____

_____

_____

_____

_____

_____

_____

_____

_____

Chapter Eight
"SWEAT SOMETIMES"

It might get tough, it might not feel good, you might have to do jobs you do not want to do, but you must press on and experience the pain of change. Anything worth having is worth working for. If it were easy, everyone would do it. Chase your passion, your vision, and your dreams, and not the money. It is okay and smart to have money, but money is for purpose, not ego; not for pride, vanity, or selfish pursuits.

I had many great examples of hard-working people in my life, such as my grandmother, my uncles, brothers, mother, and biological father. Even when I was addicted to drugs, I would often find work. My employers would praise me for my hard work but be baffled when I could not show up after I got paid during the years I was addicted to crack cocaine. I always had this intuitive nature to work extremely hard when I was on a job, and was grateful no matter what I was doing. I remember working in a warehouse as a housekeeper during my journey. I had the responsibility of keeping the bathrooms clean.

When I took the job, the bathrooms were in horrendous condition. The smell alone would make me want to throw up. However when I went to my first day of work, I wanted to get those bathrooms *so* clean because I knew my "name" was on the task. Much to my surprise, the warehouse workers were incredibly grateful to use the bathroom and feel comfortable. They told me that for many years they hated using the restroom because it appeared no one cared. Well, I did care.

No matter what job I held throughout my life, such as housekeeping, cutting football-length fields of weeds behind factories and warehouses, cleaning floors, scrubbing toilets cleaning dishes, and supervising and managing housekeeping departments, I always worked with passion and took pride in my work. I was incredibly grateful that I had the opportunity to earn money, even during the years I could not hold onto a dime due to my drug addiction.

Genesis 3:17-19–And Adam He said "Because you listened to your wife and ate the fruit, I told you not to eat, I have placed a curse on the ground. All your life you will struggle to scratch a living from it. It will grow thorns and thistles for you, though you will eat of its grains. All your life you will sweat to produce food, until your dying day. Then you will return to the ground from which you came For you were made from dust and to the dust you will return. This scripture may be a hard one to swallow, however it is truly clear that our Creator has mandated us to work. It is my belief that if this is His will for us to work, then He wants us to be grateful while living out and accepting His plan. The thorns and thistles give me clear indication that times will get tough throughout the course of our lives. However, we must continue to till the soil to produce our own fruit, since we did not accept the fruit He gave us freely.

I remember many days and nights wanting to give up while going to school, being a full-time dad and husband, a part time fitness trainer, a counselor, and interning as a drug and alcohol counselor for my doctorate degree. I cried, I sweated and I simply wanted to throw in the towel. However, I contin ued to practice gratitude while undertaking this long road of many years of education to achieve a doctorate degree with a 4.0 GPA, especially because I was delivered from addiction to crack cocaine.

I knew the odds were stacked against me because only two percent of all Americans have achieved a doctorate degree. As an African American man, the statistics are even lower and not even worthy of mention when looking at the entire population of the United States. As an African American man, I had to work ten times harder than the white population, especially in school. I noticed the higher I went in school, the less I saw people who looked like me, and the more covert acts of racism became ever so real. So hard work comes with the territory.

If you are going to make sustained changes to improve your life, particularly your financial status, you must understand that hard work and sacrifice is necessary and unfortunately depending on how you look at things, a fact of life. It is tempting to want to take the easy road, such as stealing or committing other crimes, however that is not living a sustained, useful, and whole life. Because the Creator says we will work for the rest of our days, you must simply accept that fact and be grateful when you have work. So, work hard with a great attitude and your promotion in life will come from above.

Have integrity to do what God ordered you to do when people are not around. If you work with integrity and accept the fact that the Creator mandated this fate in our lives, you will bear fruit, something he also says will happen if you sow the seed. Hard work pays off in many ways, not only in finances. It builds character, it builds self-esteem, and it fulfills the Creator's plans for mankind.

Galatians 6:3-5–For if anyone thinks he is something, when he is nothing, he deceives himself. But let each one test his own work and then his reason to boast will be in himself alone and not in his neighbor. For each will have to bear his own load. One of the many truths of our lives is the desire to have things. Often television, magazines, and social media propagate the external world and desires of the flesh. If we do not work, we will never get some of the basic things we need. Getting trapped in desires of the flesh will leave us feeling restless, irritable, and discontented when we can't achieve what we think we need.

Secondly, we become dependent on others and cannot take care of our basic needs. If you cannot take care of yourself and ruminate on ways to look for the easy way out and stay in wishful thinking, you are simply fooling yourself and reducing your self-worth. A man or woman who is living based on feelings and low self-esteem is certainly living in self-destructive thinking that will yield poor results. Unfortunately for man, the lust of the flesh and the desires of the world can be costly if we try to take short cuts in life. It is my belief that anyone who sustains their life must do it legally and with effort.

Ecclesiastes 2:9-11–So I became greater than any of the kings who ruled in Jerusalem before me. And with it all I remained clear eyed so that I could evaluate all these things. Anything I wanted, I took. I did not restrain myself from any joy, I even found great pleasure in hard work, an additional reward for all my labors. But as I looked at everything, I had worked so hard to accomplish, it was all so meaningless. In this scripture Solomon describes how he found great pleasure in hard work, but in the end even our hard work is meaningless without being in God's will.

If you truly look at this scripture, when he says "find pleasure in hard work" there is a powerful implication that this is the will of the Creator, and we should accept this as a fact of life. If you don't like the work that you do, let me remind you that you can stay grateful while you do that work. Most importantly, you can overcome complacency and fear, and try and achieve whatever education, contacts, or other resources to do work you will like.

Solomon also makes it clear that *"dreaming all the time instead of working is foolishness" (Ecclesiastes 5:7)*. His words about everything we do being meaningless and futile at the end of the day do not mean that nothing we do matters, but rather imply that life lived solely for our will, without a relationship with the Creator who made you and has a purpose and meaning for you, is in fact meaningless.

Proverbs 14:23–In all toil there is profit, but mere talk tends only to poverty. I want to expound on this scripture. When you define the word "toil" it means to work hard or incessantly. Again, the scriptures confirm that our duty to work hard and find pleasure in our work is a part of our humanity that is necessary, but more importantly God's will. If it is His will as I know it is, then we must accept it and know that He watches us when we work.

I have embraced this factor in my life, and I simply make sure that whatever job I have to do, I work unto the Lord. If you want something different in life, then you must do something different. Working hard is a fact of life. There is no easy way out, even though some get the pleasure of having enough money to make things easier, somebody paid the price and eventually the one who does nothing will pay the price in another way.

Think about it this way. If you are born into wealth and have no appreciation for hard work, then the price might be pride, selfish pursuits of happiness, and low self-worth hiding behind money you never earned or worked for. Either way, some part of self will be affected, whether mental, emotional, physical, or spiritual if you do not grasp the fact that we are mandated to work.

1 Thessalonians 4:11-12–And to aspire to live quietly, and to mind your own affairs, and to work with your hands, as we instructed you, so that you may walk properly before outsiders and be dependent on no one. Lastly, I want to inspire you to work hard so you can be independent and not dependent. One of the best feelings in the world is to not feel dependent on someone to take care of your basic needs.

People who consistently use the welfare system and become dependent on that money without recognizing that our Father in Heaven makes it very clear that we must work are simply living in fear, lethargy, and victimization. The welfare system should simply be used as a temporary relief while people develop and create ways to become independent. This means work, hard work. I have interpreted that "walking properly before outsiders" means being a role model of hard work, to inspire others to do the same.

» Are you working in your purpose and if not, why? Are you settling for the security of a steady paycheck and or some other income source and dreaming about what you want to do? (Explain.)

_____

_____

_____

_____

_____

_____

_____

_____

_____

_____

_____

_____

_____

_____

_____

_____

_____

_____

_____

_____

_____

_____

» Do you work with integrity while no one is looking? If not, why not? If so, how does it improve how you feel about yourself, others, and your spirit?

_____

_____

_____

_____

_____

_____

_____

_____

_____

_____

_____

_____

_____

_____

_____

_____

_____

_____

_____

_____

_____

_____

_____

_____

Chapter Nine
"DON'T WASTE THINKING"

Honor and respect your craft, your gifts, and the world around you. Stay humble and open-minded enough to gain new knowledge about unknown people, places, and things. Remember your perception and knowledge is based on your own experiences and culture. We all have individual cultures and experiences. The world is big and diverse, just because you have a gift does not mean you know everything about it. Develop it, nurture it, and respect it. You may not want to attend college or a university, but if you desire to grow as a person there must be an intention to learn more about life and other experiences, otherwise it will be hard to empathize and create community with people. Stinking thinking will shut us off from the world outside and trap us in our own "box," if you will. How can you grow as a person without being intentional to learn what you don't know?

Ecclesiastes 10:10 states that *"since a dull ax requires great strength, sharpen the blade. That the value of wisdom it helps you succeed."* Sharpening the blade means recognizing where a problem exists, acquiring the skills or tools to do the job better, and then going out and doing it. Find areas of your life where your "ax" is dull and sharpen your skills so you can be more effective for God's work and live out your purpose, whatever that may be for you.

According to *The 7 Principles of Highly Effective People,*

most of our mental development and study discipline comes through formal education. But as soon as we leave the external discipline of school, many of us let our minds atrophy. We do not do any serious reading; we do not explore new subjects in any real depth. We do not think analytically, we do not write—at least not in a way that tests our ability to express ourselves in distilled, clear, and concise language. Instead, we spend our time watching television.

I might add that if you do not expand your knowledge base it is extremely easy to go about our lives making assumptions, forming biases, stereotyping, and categorizing people based on one point of view: our own. It becomes extremely easy to become stagnated, which subsequently keeps you in a selfish state, only looking for ways to make yourself feel better or groveling in self-pity.

Once I was delivered from my addiction and started the process of examining myself, I realized that my world and how I saw things was extremely limited. I was given advice to acquire new knowledge by reading the Bible more often, reading self-help books, listening to and being around driven people, going to Twelve Step meetings and reading the material, and simply being open-minded to new ideas. Although I do not attend Twelve Step meetings on a regular basis or utilize the process for my spiritual development now, I learned so much about myself during the times in my life that I attended.

When I decided to overcome my fear and go back to college, my view of the world and myself changed dramatically. I know college might not be for everyone, but I promise you getting an education was one of the most profound experiences that built my self-esteem, opened my eyes to my ignorance (lack of knowledge), gave me new hope, and helped me to accept the differences in people and the world. At the very least read, learn to read if you cannot read, and make sure whatever you read is material that will give you new insight and understanding of yourself and the world around you. Simply remember how I described "culture" in Chapter Three. Remember we all have acquired knowledge based on many variables, especially from our culture.

The world we live in and the people we meet every day are complex. If you do not purposely look to expand your knowledge in some form, whether formal education or other avenues, you will simply continue to operate in some form of self-destructive thinking and behavior. If all you know about a certain ethnic group of people is based on media, your living environment, or limited information about them, it is very easy to form assumptions and respond with bigotry, racism, biases, or unfairness, due to your limited knowledge. When I took sociology classes, I realized firsthand how I also formed opinions about whole groups of people based on my limited view of the world and my multicultural ignorance.

Getting knowledge and expanding your horizons is essential if you are going to overcome self-destructive thinking. If you have hate, envy, jealousy, unkind thoughts about others, unforgiveness in your heart, or if you have biases and make assumptions about people, you are in self-destructive thinking, and will invariably see negative outcomes, even if it's as simple as not showing kindness or respect. I learned that this factor was especially important for me to develop relationships, to learn how to communicate effectively, and to have the ability to show love and tolerance. This factor made me a better employee, father, husband, and person.

» What are you doing to increase your awareness of life, people, and current events, and why is it important? (Explain.)

_____

_____

_____

_____

_____

_____

_____

_____

_____

_____

_____

_____

_____

_____

_____

_____

_____

_____

_____

_____

_____

_____

_____

» How does knowledge help you transform and sustain change in all areas of your life?

» Is fear, procrastination, or laziness keeping you from expanding your horizons? (Explain.) If not, explain what you do to continue to develop healthy thinking?

Chapter Ten
"LOVE YOURSELF"

We cannot control people, places, things, or events. However, we have the power to accept reality even when we do not get our way. *Philippians 4:6* says, *"do not worry about anything, instead pray about everything. Tell God what you need and thank Him for all he has done."* This process can be much harder than you think. Often our expectations of people and events can leave us feeling resentful and angry because we simply want things our way and they do not go the way we want them to.

If we do not understand ourselves and our motives, it is quite easy for our feelings to run the show. If you are making decisions based on what you are feeling, the idea of acceptance and practicing acceptance will be precarious at best. Without practicing acceptance, you will surely be restless, irritable, and discontented to some degree.

However, the principle of acceptance is facing the reality that whether we accept things with a positive attitude or a negative attitude, it does not negate the outcome. Being powerless can really "suck," for lack of a better term. However, even if we do not have a choice in the outcomes of what people say and do, or how events turn out, we do have the choice to maintain gratitude and a friendly attitude. So, what do you choose? To be at peace, or to be discontented? In other words, you do have a choice to accept things with a friendly attitude.

I often tell people that I help, if your expectations are high, you will have proportionally lower serenity and peace. You simply do not have power to control things outside of you. Your center of power is within you and that is truly the only power you have. Yes, our ideas of power can often be delusional. For example, your superior at work might be in a position of "power" and you have no control over how they respond, react, or communicate. However, you have a choice in how you respond. You can either accept their way of behaving with a great attitude and practice some assertiveness in your communication to hopefully get your voice heard, or you could walk off the job and deal with the consequences (which may lead to you being empowered to look for a new job). So while the superior has power to influence, the superior cannot control you.

Practicing acceptance is also in line with having faith. You continue to strive, achieve, learn, and understand that the outcomes are simply not up to you. You may have a desire for something, and you may even set a goal to achieve that desire. But when life shows up, and trust me it will, what you expected might not happen. In my book *Faith to Freedom: From Dumpster to Doctor*, I talked about wanting to play professional football early in the story. I did everything I could to achieve that goal.

However, the dangers of the sport and the risks of injury destroyed that dream. It took me years to simply accept the fact that my Creator had something else in mind. No matter how hard I tried to overcome the physical and mental disruptions the injury had on me, I simply could not play football again. I know you the reader more than likely had dreams desires, and expectations that got disrupted, and that hurt or disappointed you. If you are honest, you probably allowed some of those disappointments to disrupt you to some degree, even if it was as simple as being in a state of depression or projecting anger or a bad attitude on others without them realizing what was going on in your world.

Practicing acceptance and not passing blame was one of the hardest factors for me to apply, but one of the most important, especially in the process of forgiving others and what happened to me in the past. In the process of practicing acceptance, I had to learn to forgive myself and my limitations and smash my fear-driven ego that constantly sought validation and approval. However it is by far one of the most liberating and profound factors. When we forgive others who have hurt us and accept that our Creator allowed everything that took place in our lives to happen, and that He makes no mistakes, we can learn and begin to understand how our situations lead us to His purpose.

So, consider how futile and meaningless it is to not accept events that took place and are happening daily that we cannot control. Today you might have to consider forgiveness to move on. Being a victim is seriously a decision and an excuse to not take responsibility for your life and live out your purpose. Did you ever consider that your pain from the past and your present struggles have been something that are allowed to happen by the Creator for the purpose of teaching and shaping you, for His purpose not yours?

Yes, I imagine that life would be great if everything could happen just as my perfection would want it to. Unfortunately, we are human, and we all have limitations. We will invariably fall short of our own expectations, and be critical of others who do not live up to our expectations. One thing I will prom ise you: if you do not practice acceptance you will always be in a state of discontentment and the bondage of self. You will not experience the freedom to live as the authentic you.

Let me give you another example of acceptance. Let us say a friend or spouse is verbally abusive towards you, which leaves you feeling low and very hurt. You may not be able to change that person, but you have the power to change the situation. To find your peace and continue to build your own self-esteem acceptance in this situation may take a few steps to get this person to change their behaviors towards you. You might have to practice setting boundaries and loving yourself enough to practice assertive communications, get some coun seling by an objective outside party, or even leave that person However, at the end of the day, unless you set the boundary even if it might lead to severing the relationship, you will continue to stay discontented or angry to some degree. And if you are angry, hurt, or discontented, there is no acceptance

Acceptance is all about attitude. If I am at some level of peace and serenity during any disturbance that I have no power to control, and I have the ability to show love, tole ance, and kindness, then that's a clear sign of accepting events as they are in that moment. Remember the most important principle of practicing acceptance is your power to change "you." If the situation is outside your center of influence, you must consider what you can do to find your peace and seren ity and to be more useful and whole.

The *Twelve and Twelve* of Alcohol Anonymous states that most human disturbances can be linked to human instincts that are used beyond their intended purpose. I would add that if your instincts are used beyond their intended purpose then your ability to practice acceptance will also be compromised and undoubtedly leave you restless, irritable, or discontented. We all have instincts for social connectedness and emotional security. If you are very insecure about yourself, you must understand that your instincts are still working, which means when you are seeking connection with other people, you will often feel disturbed and unable to accept that person if they are not validating you.

The verbal and non-verbal expressions you perceive from others will have power to stimulate fear and insecurity based on your own thinking. If your inner self-talk (which is often unconscious) is negative, you will undoubtedly be challenged daily to quiet your instincts for emotional security and social connectedness and have trouble accepting people as they are.

I had to learn through my journey of self-discovery that I had to change the faulty belief system I operated under in order to find peace and accept my powerlessness to control what I have no control over. For example, if someone has an opinion about something that is different than yours, it is absolutely senseless to stay restless, irritable, and discontented with them when you have no power to change them. Even if you do not agree, the one thing you have power to do is respond by practicing acceptance.

The more I forgave myself and developed love for myself by overcoming my fears and doing healthy things that not only nurtured me but also served others, the easier it became for me to practice acceptance. As I grew to love and understand myself and what being powerless means in context with other people, it became easier to set boundaries with people who hurt me or walk away if necessary, and accept where they are in their life.

I realized that if I practiced being assertive, caring, and forgiving, and they decided to change their negative behaviors towards me, then I could accept them, and our love and friendship could grow. If things did not work out after I communicated with them assertively and they continued to violate my healthy boundaries, acceptance at that point might mean me practicing the courage and faith to love myself enough to leave the situation, and accept only that I deserve to be loved and respected.

It might hurt to leave a situation that you adapted and became accustomed to, but if that situation does not affirm you in a healthy manner, it is your faulty thinking, not theirs that keeps you in an unhealthy situation. Practicing acceptance has many variables, but one thing is for sure, if you cannot accept something, you can change how you respond and what you decide to do to find your serenity.

1 Thessalonians 5:11–Therefore encourage one another and build one another up, just as you are doing. This scripture inspired me to listen, learn, and accept other people and what they are going through, so I could continue to better my life and be an inspiration. I had to learn about their dreams and vision for themselves. When we are stagnating in isolation (thinking only of ourselves) being of service to others and building up others is impossible, because it becomes all about you.

Philippians 2:4–Let each of you look not only to his own interests, but also to the interests of others. One of the most profound and rewarding experiences I have had in my life is the ability to learn from my past mistakes and use what I learned to encourage, inspire, and help others. Helping others can be a diversion from feeling stagnant. Being stagnant in life is not the intention of our Creator. While in the process of recrea ing my life, I discovered that the more I helped and accepted others, the more I helped myself.

Serving others and practicing acceptance on a consistent basis takes the "power" out of our selfish human nature. Instead of everything being about ourselves and what we desire, the practice of service and acceptance brings a sense of meaning, gratitude, and balance back our lives. Service will lift your spirit and build your esteem. Practicing being of service and accepting life as it is, especially that which I have no power to change, has a way of bringing purpose and stimulating new commitment to your life.

When I was in my first few years of freedom from drugs, I was so grateful for the deliverance from the grip of addiction, I would get up every morning to attend an early meeting at the Union Station Homeless Shelter. Each morning this shelter would feed the occupants of the shelter and have a one hour meeting focused on discussions about life, the next step in life, goals in life, and other topics to stimulate growth and awareness. Not every person at the shelter was there due to drug addiction. Many had fallen on hard times, some suffered mental health challenges, and some simply appeared to be giving up on life.

I often had the chance to speak about issues and struggles, and encourage others. The more I went to the shelter, the more some of the occupants who were there for months using all the resources and services of the shelter would feel disappointed or actually tell me that they missed me on the days that I did not show up. For the first time in years, people began to count on me and desire my input.

The experience at the shelter humbled me to see life through other people's eyes and helped me to stay grateful.

More importantly, for the first time in many years my life took on new meaning, making a positive impact and giving love to the universe instead of being selfish and inconsiderate. The process of helping others and practicing acceptance continued to build my self-esteem, and drove me to get more creative to grow and develop, so I could give back to the world.

The sense of loneliness and despair left me. Being of service, accepting and having empathy towards others had the power to stimulate new thinking in me, and I was able to actually witness others' smiles for the first time in a long time. I was able to hear others thank me for being in their lives, hear them say they desired to get up and not give up due to watching me grow. It is amazing how much influence we can have on others just by changing ourselves and practicing unselfish behaviors that serve others with no motives.

Michael Jackson's song "Man in the Mirror" says it best. If you want to make a change in the world, take look at the "man in the mirror" and change him first. Being of service and accepting others forces you to look at yourself, and it has a way of helping you gain an intuitive way of handling situations which may have baffled you in the past (e.g., placing others' needs in front of your own, or not blaming others for your lack of love for yourself) because you are now thinking of others and not just yourself.

» Write examples of how you can show love to yourself when you are practicing acceptance and being of service to others? What are the positive impacts that it could have transforming your mind, body, and spirit?

Notes

For Speaking Engagements, Book Signings,
Appearances, and Interviews...

Dedicato Treatment Center Inc.
22 West Carter Avenue
Sierra Madre, CA 91024

Office (626) 921-0113

Cell   (626) 644-8857

klm196227@gmail.com

www.dedicatedtreatment.com

facebook.com/klm196227

Made in the USA
Las Vegas, NV
01 November 2020